My New
Dad

By Jillian Powell
Photography by Bobby Humphrey

WAYLAND

First published in 2011 by Wayland

Copyright © Wayland 2011

Wayland
338 Euston Road
London NW1 3BH

Wayland Australia
Level 17/207 Kent Street
Sydney, NSW 2000

Editor, Wayland: Julia Adams
Produced for Wayland by Discovery Books Ltd
Managing editor: Rachel Tisdale
Project editor: Colleen Ruck
Designer: Ian Winton
Photography: Bobby Humphrey
Consultant: Helen Beale (Teacher and Library Coordinator,
Robert Le Kyng Primary School, Swindon)

The author and photographer would like to acknowledge the
following for their help in preparing this book: Kevin, Julie, Peter,
Matthew and Milly Morris; Harry Dewar; Ruby Burrows.

British Library Cataloguing in Publication Data
 Powell, Jillian.
   My new dad.
   1. Stepparents--Pictorial works--Juvenile literature.
   I. Title
   306.8'747-dc22

ISBN: 978 0 7502 6287 3

Printed in China

Wayland is a division of Hachette Children's Books, an Hachette UK company.
www.hachette.co.uk

Contents

My family

My name is Milly.
I have a brother
called Matthew
and we have a
dog called Fern.

We live with Mum and our new
step-dad, Kevin. He moved in
with us a few months ago.

Moving in

Matthew and I first got to know Kevin when he started going out with Mum. He used to come to visit.

Sometimes we went to the park together at the weekend.

Kevin often came to stay. Then Mum told us he was moving in with us. On the day, Matthew and I made space for his things and helped him **unpack**.

Changes

When Mum told me Kevin was moving in I felt upset at first. I was used to it being just Mum, Matthew and me.

Mum said when things change it is always a bit scary at first. She told me we are going to have lots of fun as a family together.

Kevin says that he really loves my mum. He **promises** that Matthew and I will still get to spend lots of time with her.

Helping us

Kevin is really clever at **mending** things around the house.
He fixes my bike for me.

In the evening, Kevin helps us with
our homework. Kevin says we can
always ask him when we need help.

Kevin's son

Kevin has a son called Harry. Harry lives with his mum. He often comes to our house to spend time with his dad.

Harry is our **step-brother**. Sometimes we all go to the park. Harry is the same age as Matthew and they like playing together.

Weekends

Harry comes to stay with us some weekends. He often brings his bike so we can ride around together in the garden.

When the weather is nice we
go to the playing fields.

We take a picnic
for lunch.

Family arguments

Sometimes when the boys are playing they start **arguing** over a toy or a game. Kevin says we all have to learn to get along now we are a family.

I get cross when Kevin tells me
off or tells me to tidy my bedroom.
He is not really my dad.

But Mum says we have to listen to him.
Even though Kevin is not our real dad,
he still loves and cares for us like a dad.

Having fun

Mum is happy that Kevin is living with us, and Matthew and I like it, too.

Kevin has some really good computer games. We have lots of fun playing on them together.

Kevin always says that exercise is good for us. He teaches Matthew and me some football tricks. It is fun!

My step-family

I am getting used to having a new dad now. Some of my friends at school have step-dads, too. I can talk to them about my new family.

Having a step-dad means you have two families, really. Matthew and I have more family and friends to play with now.

Glossary

arguing having a row with each other.

mending fixing something.

promise If you promise to do something, you say that you will definitely do it.

step-brother son of your step-mum or step-dad.

step-dad father through partnership or marriage, rather than birth.

unpack take things out of a bag or box.

Further information

Books

Meet the Family: My Dad by Mary Auld (Franklin Watts, 2008)

Popcorn: Families: My Dad by Katie Dicker (Wayland, 2010)

Thoughts and Feelings: Our Stepfamily by Julie Johnson (Franklin Watts, 2007)

Websites

www.childline.org.uk/Explore/HomeFamilies/Pages/Stepfamilies.aspx
This website looks at what it is like to be part of a step-family.

www.cyh.com
The Kids' Health section of this website includes helpful information about topics including step-families, family relationships and family conflict.

www.kidshealth.org/kid/feeling
Practical advice on issues affecting step-families including getting used to step-parents and what to do if you can't get along.

Things to do

Speaking and listening
Do your friends at school have a step-parent? Talk to them about how they feel about it. Have their feelings changed over time? If you have a step-brother or step-sister, talk to them about how they feel about their new family. Do you share some of the same feelings?

Art
Collect some photos of your family members to make a scrap book. Make a collage for each family member about what they like and dislike. Cut out pictures from magazines and newspapers and stick them onto coloured card.

Numeracy
Count how many people in your class have a step-parent. They might have a step-brother or step-sister, too.

Index

My New

Contents of titles in series:

Childminder
978 0 7502 6288 0

My family
My new childminder
After school
At the park
Playing indoors
Arts and crafts
Dinner time
Having fun
Home with Mum

Friend
978 0 7502 6286 6

My home
Neighbours
Classmates
Visiting Emily
Playing together
Not friends?
Together again
Emily's birthday
The party

Sister
978 0 7502 6285 9

My family
Shopping for baby
Getting ready
Mum goes to hospital
My sister Holly
Helping out
At home with my sister
Playtime
Bath and bedtime

Dad
978 0 7502 6287 3

My family
Moving in
Changes
Helping us
Kevin's son
Weekends
Family arguments
Having fun
My step-family

School
978 0 7502 6284 2

My first day at school
My class
Assembly
Paint and play
Snack time
Reading and writing
Lunch
Circle time
Going home

WAYLAND